W9-BNB-096

VENUS

A TRUE BOOK

by

Larry Dane Brimner

Children's Press®
A Division of Grolier Publishing

New York London Hong Kong Sydney
Danbury, Connecticut

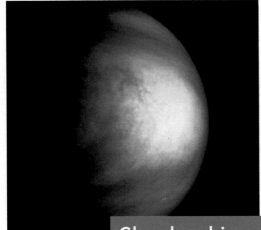

Clouds whip around Venus.

Subject Consultant
Peter Goodwin
Science Department Chairman
Kent School, Kent, CT

Reading Consultant
Linda Cornwell
Learning Resource Consultant
Indiana Department
of Education

Author's Dedication:
For my friends at
Austin's Barton Creek
Elementary School

Visit Children's Press® on the Internet at:
http://publishing.grolier.com

Library of Congress Cataloging-in-Publication Data

Brimner, Larry Dane.
   Venus / by Larry Dane Brimner.
      p. cm. — (A true book)
   Includes bibliographical references and index.
   Summary: Discusses our early ideas about the planet Venus, what we
have discovered about its true nature, and what we may learn from it in
the future.
   ISBN 0-516-21158-7 (lib.bdg.)   0-516-26443-5 (pbk.)
   1. Venus (Planet)—Juvenile literature. [1. Venus (Planet)] I. Title.
II. Series.
QB621.B745 1998
523.42—dc21   97-52144
                                                              CIP
                                                              AC

© 1998 by Larry Dane Brimner
All rights reserved. Published simultaneously in Canada
Printed in the United States of America
1 2 3 4 5 6 7 8 9 10 R 07 06 05 04 03 02 01 00 99 98

Contents

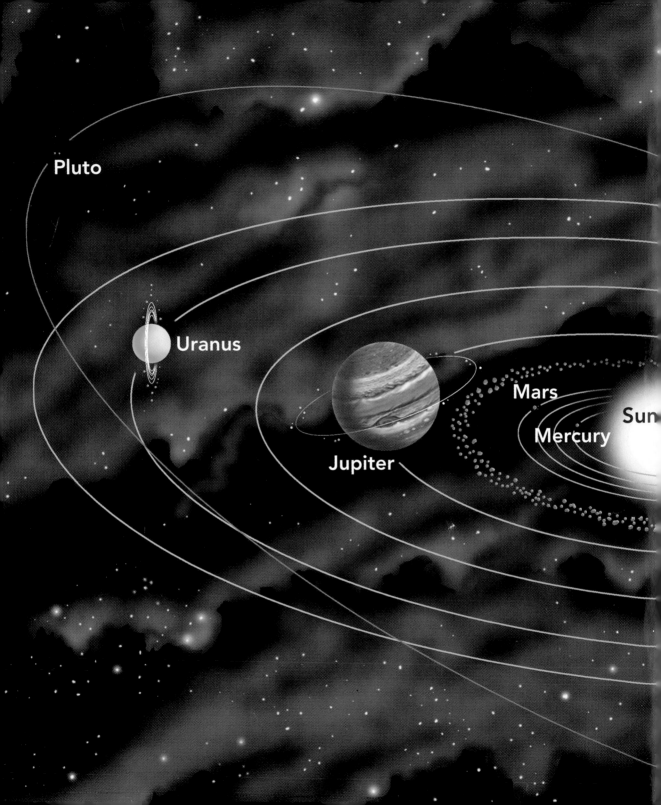

The Solar System

Venus

Moon

Earth

Asteroid Belt

Saturn

Neptune

Jewel of the Sky

Venus is like no other planet in the solar system. If you look up at the night sky, you can see that Venus seems to outshine all the other planets. Only the Sun and Moon look brighter than Venus. People call Venus the "jewel of the sky" because

Venus (top) and the Moon (bottom) are two of the brightest objects in the night sky.

Because people thought the planet Venus was so beautiful, they named it after the Roman goddess of love and beauty.

of the way it seems to glow. Ancient people named Venus for the Roman goddess of love and beauty.

Sometimes, Venus is low in the evening sky. It seems to follow the setting Sun. At other times, you can see it in the morning sky before the Sun rises. This has made Venus an object of wonder to early sky watchers as well as to modern astronomers.

Old Ideas

When early sky watchers saw Venus in the night sky, they called it the "evening star." When they saw Venus in the morning sky, they called it the "morning star." They thought Venus was two separate objects.

The Sun, the brightest object in the sky, was worshiped by

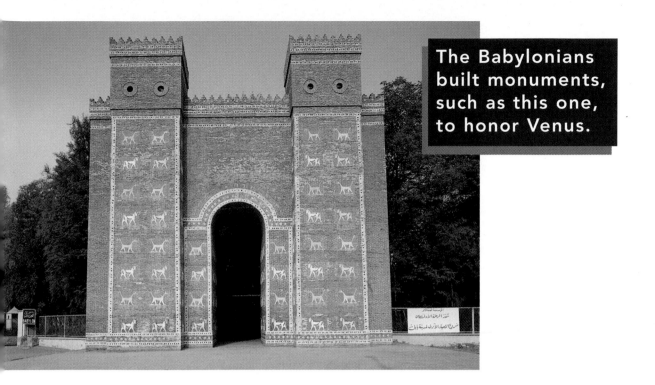

The Babylonians built monuments, such as this one, to honor Venus.

early people. Venus seemed to follow the Sun, or it appeared in the sky just before the Sun came up. So Venus was also important in many early religions. The Babylonians, who lived in what is now Iraq, thought Venus was the mother of all the gods. They built great temples to honor her.

The Maya people of Central America believed that Venus was the Sun's brother. When the Sun and Venus set in the evening, the Maya thought the brothers had gone into a dark underworld to fight against evil. If they won the battle, Venus would rise in the sky as the morning star to announce their victory, and the Sun would follow.

These Sun god masks were carved by the Maya people.

Of course, today we know that Venus is neither a mother nor a warrior, and it is one object, not two. Like Earth, Venus is a planet. "Planet" is a word that means "wanderer."

Looking Closer at Venus

In the 1600s, astronomers used the first telescopes to get a better look at the sky. The Italian astronomer Galileo Galilei (1564–1642) discovered that Venus has phases just like our Moon. Only one side of Venus it lit by the Sun at a

Galileo used his telescope to study Venus.

Venus goes through phases,
just like our Moon.

time. Phases occur when we see different amounts of the lit side of the planet. So to observers on Earth, Venus seems to change shape.

The early telescopes also showed that Venus is surrounded by thick clouds. Because the Sun's light bounces off the clouds, Venus seems brighter than other planets. But the clouds also blocked a clear view of Venus's surface. What was Venus like under the clouds?

Twin Planets

Astronomers had many ideas about Venus, even though they could not see below its clouds. They thought Venus and Earth were very much alike.

Both planets are about the same size. Venus is 7,516 miles (12,100 kilometers) wide. Earth is only a little bigger. Venus's

Even the most powerful telescopes cannot look beneath Venus's clouds.

year is almost as long as Earth's. It takes Venus 225 Earth-days, or one Venus year, to travel around the Sun. It

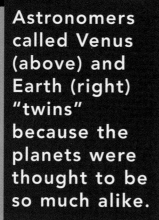

Astronomers called Venus (above) and Earth (right) "twins" because the planets were thought to be so much alike.

takes Earth 365 days to orbit the Sun. Venus is the second planet from the Sun and Earth is the third. So Venus and Earth are neighbors. Venus was nicknamed Earth's "twin" because Venus and Earth are so much alike.

In the 1960s, however, astronomers discovered that Venus and Earth are not twins. A planet rotates, or spins, on its axis. An axis is an imaginary line that runs between a planet's north and south poles. It is daytime on the side of the planet that is lit by the Sun, and nighttime on the side that is in darkness. It takes Earth 24 hours—one day—to spin once. Scientists discovered that Venus spins much slower—only once every 243 Earth-days! Venus also spins in the opposite direction of most planets. If you were on Venus, you would see the Sun rise in the west and set in the east.

Touching Down

Venera 7 was the first spacecraft to successfully land on another planet. Launched by the Soviet Union in August 1970, it landed on Venus in December 1970. It sent photos and other information back to Earth for 23 minutes.

A photo of Venus's surface (above) taken from *Venera 7* (right)

What We Know

The United States and the
Soviet Union (now Russia)
began to send probes, or
spacecraft, into space in the
early 1960s. From these
probes, we learned more
about Venus than ever before.
Mariner 2 was the first probe
to study Venus. It sent back

information telling us that Venus is a harsh world—the harshest in the solar system. Its average temperature is a scorching 870 degrees Fahrenheit (465 degrees Celsius). That's hot enough to melt lead!

Because clouds on Earth are made up of water, astronomers thought Venus's clouds might be made of water, too. Since water is necessary for plants and animals to survive, astronomers believed there might be life on Venus, just as there is on Earth.

But *Mariner 2* showed scientists that Venus's clouds do not contain water. The clouds formed from droplets of sulfuric acid, a substance that would kill humans. Some astronomers believe there was once water on Venus, but the *Magellan* space probe, launched in 1989,

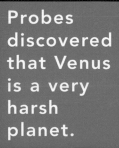

Probes
discovered
that Venus
is a very
harsh
planet.

The *Magellan* space probe
starts out on its journey.

found no signs of past water. Venus's atmosphere (the gases that surround Venus) has little oxygen—a gas people need to survive. It is mostly carbon dioxide, one of the gases people breathe out of their bodies.

Venus is lifeless, but it is still a very interesting planet. At the upper levels of Venus's clouds, the wind whips around at 217 miles per hour (350 km per hour).

Venus's surface has flat plains and high mountains.

On Venus's surface, which is mostly rock, there is almost no wind. There are flat areas called plains and high areas with mountains. Maxwell Montes is the highest mountain on Venus. It is a little higher than Mount Everest, Earth's tallest peak. Venus is also home to Baltis Vallis, the solar system's longest known "river." No water flows in Baltis Vallis, but the channel is more than 4,200 miles

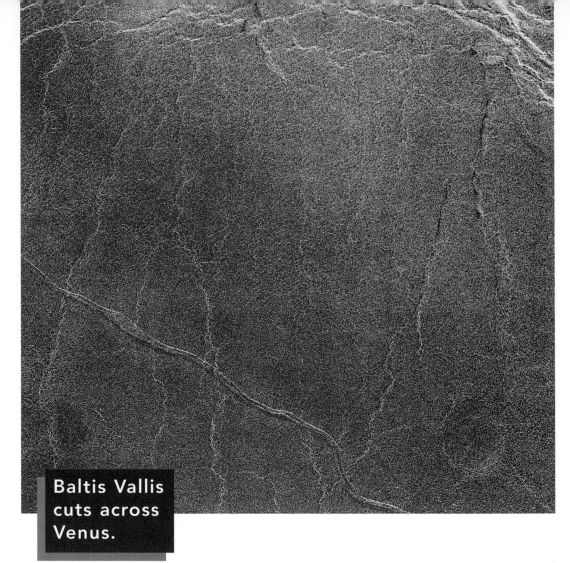

Baltis Vallis cuts across Venus.

(6,760 km) long—longer than two of Earth's greatest rivers, the Amazon and Nile.

Lessons from Venus

Venus is hot and unable to support living things. Even so, many scientists continue to think that Venus and Earth were once very similar. If this is true, what happened to change Venus?

Some scientists believe that Venus changed because it

Greenhouses do not let heat escape. This makes the temperature inside very warm.

might act like a giant greenhouse. A greenhouse lets in
the Sun's heat, but keeps
most of it from escaping. This
makes the greenhouse warm,
even when it is cool outside.

Scientists think that
Venus's layers of clouds and
the carbon dioxide in its
atmosphere allow heat to
enter but keep it from escaping back into space. Over
time, Venus has become hotter and hotter.

If it is true that Venus changed from a pleasant planet into a harsh one, it may be a lesson for us. Usually, planets change over billions of years. Earth has changed over time, too, but some scientists worry that humans might be causing Earth to change rapidly.

Factories burning fuel and exhaust from cars create more carbon dioxide and make the air dirty. This

If we are not careful, Earth's hot summers could get even hotter!

polluted air may be causing Earth to hold in heat and get warmer, like a greenhouse. If we are not careful, we may change our planet so much that it will no longer be able to support living things.

Scientists think they can learn a lot from Venus. Venus may help them discover more about the solar system and why there seems to be no life on other planets. Probes will study Venus.

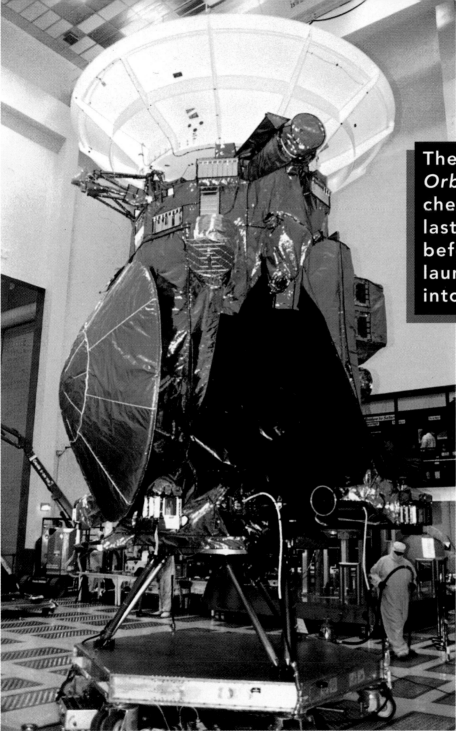

The *Cassini Orbiter* was checked one last time before it was launched into space.

One of them, the *Cassini Orbiter,* was launched in October 1997. The *Cassini Orbiter* will pass by Venus twice as it builds up speed for its trip to Saturn in 2004. These passes may tell us more about Venus—the jewel of the sky—and perhaps more about the future of Earth.

The *Magellan* spacecraft mapped Venus's surface, but there is even more information for new probes to discover.

Venus Quick Facts

Diameter	7,516 miles (12,100 km)
Average distance from the Sun	67.2 million miles (108 million km)
Average surface temperature	870°F (465°C)
Length of day	243 Earth-days
Length of year	225 Earth-days
Moons	None

Missions to Venus

Mission	Launch Date
Mariner 2 (USA)	August 27, 1962
Venera 4 (Soviet Union)	June 12, 1967
Venera 7 (Soviet Union)	August 17, 1970
Mariner 10 (USA)	November 3, 1973
Venera 9 (Soviet Union)	June 8, 1975
Magellan (USA)	May 4, 1989
Cassini Orbiter (USA and Europe)	October 15, 1997

To Find Out More

Here are more places to learn about Venus and other planets in space:

 **Books**

Branley, Franklyn. **Venus: Magellan Explores Our Twin Planets.** HarperCollins, 1994.

Brewer, Duncan. **Venus.** Marshall Cavendish, 1993.

Schloss, Muriel. **Venus.** Franklin Watts, 1991.

Simon, Seymour. **Venus.** Morrow Junior Books, 1992.

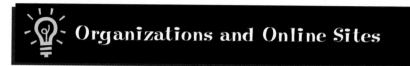

Organizations and Online Sites

The Children's Museum of Indianapolis

3000 N. Meridian Street
Indianapolis, IN 46208-4716
(317) 924-5431
*http://childrensmuseum.org/
sq1.htm*

Visit the SpaceQuest Planetarium to see what it has to offer, including a view of this month's night sky.

National Aeronautics and Space Administration (NASA)

http://www.nasa.gov

At NASA's home page, you can access information about its exciting history and present resources and missions.

National Air and Space Museum

Smithsonian Institution
601 Independence Ave. SW
Washington, DC 20560
(202) 357-1300
http://www.nasm.si.edu/

The National Air and Space Museum site gives you up-to-date information about its programs and exhibits.

The Nine Planets

*http://seds.lpl.arizona.edu/
nineplanets/nineplanets/*

Take a multimedia tour of the solar system and all its planets and moons.

Space Telescope Science Institute

3700 San Martin Drive
Johns Hopkins University
Homewood Campus
Baltimore, MD 21218
(410) 338-4700
http://www.stsci.edu//

The Space Telescope Science Institute operates the Hubble Space Telescope. Visit this site to see pictures of the telescope's outer-space view.

Windows to the Universe

*http://windows.engin.
umich.edu/*

This site lets you click on all nine planets to find information about each one. It also covers many other space subjects, including important historical figures, scientists, and astronauts.

Important Words

astronomer a scientist who studies objects in space

atmosphere the gases that surround a planet

axis an imaginary line about which a planet turns

orbit to travel around an object

phases when we see different amounts of the side of a planet that is lit by the Sun

probe a spacecraft used to study space

rotate to spin

telescope an instrument that makes faraway objects look closer

Index

Meet the Author

Larry Dane Brimner taught school for twenty years and is now a full-time writer. He is the author of more than fifty books for young readers, including *Max and Felix*; *Merry Christmas, Old Armadillo*; and these other titles in the True Book series: *E-Mail*, *The World Wide Web*, and *The Winter Olympics*.

Photographs ©: Art Resource: 13 (Danielle Gustafson), 8; Itar-Tass/Sovofoto: 23 bottom; NASA: 20 top (JPL), cover, 1, 16, 20 bottom, 27, 28, 30, 32, 41, 42, 43; Photo Researchers: 34 (Renee Lynn), 2 (Mark Marten), 15 (Mary Evans Picture Library), 39 (NASA/SPL), 7 (Pekka Parviainen); Superstock, Inc.: 11; The Planetary System /Astron Society of the Pacific: 23 top; Tony Stone Images: 19 (Scott Goldsmith); Viesti Collection, Inc.: 37 (Frank Siteman).

Diagram on pages 4-5 by Greg Harris.